Mukedi Diesta-Mputu Delphin

VIRUSES IN THE COMPUTER WORLD

Mukedi Diesta-Mputu Delphin

VIRUSES IN THE COMPUTER WORLD

ScienciaScripts

Imprint

Cover image: www.ingimage.com

This book is a translation from the original published under ISBN 978-620-6-72494-0.

Publisher:
Sciencia Scripts
is a trademark of
Dodo Books Indian Ocean Ltd. and OmniScriptum S.R.L publishing group

120 High Road, East Finchley, London, N2 9ED, United Kingdom
Str. Armeneasca 28/1, office 1, Chisinau MD-2012, Republic of Moldova, Europe
Printed at: see last page
ISBN: 978-620-8-26464-2

DEDICATION

To all my offspring, the Diesta-Mputu dynasty;

To all Men of God,

To all the communities of higher education institutions and universities, ... which benefit from my support,

To all of you.

I dedicate this manual to you.

ACKNOWLEDGEMENTS

The drafting of a scientific paper requires the collaboration of several people, some of whom are directly involved and others: the heroes in the shadows, whom we can never forget.

Viruses in the computer world have only gone this way, and we admit it.

To my various collaborators in general and in particular: Willy Lakungu, Jean-Baptiste Mimbu, Donat Bobia, Carine Ngiengi, Mfutila Chimène Ngunda, Nkutu Pelagie;

To all my offspring: "The Mukedi dynasty".

To the late Ilunga Placide, Charles Ndeke, Pépe, Flavien Mayibanzila and Akemito Malu Constant ... above all, they gave me a taste for teaching in Higher and University Education.

I would like to express my sincere gratitude to all those in charge of Bircham International University (BIU), who have given me this great house of Editions Universitaires Européennes, which is my 3ème cycle institution.

To Professor Wani Ley Florent, the historian, to Professor Pezo Nassou Rigobert (le tata longi ya nene), our great and long-standing comrade in struggle, whom we can never forget, and our loyalty in collaboration remains our one and only dividend.

To all those responsible for Editions Universitaires Européennes: in particular Mrs Ecaterina Foghel, Mr El Hajji...

I would also like to express my gratitude to all those whose names are not included on this page, who have contributed in any way to the success of this work.

Please accept my indelible affection for your various encouraging contributions to making this thought available to everyone.

Preamble

The gnashing of teeth that IT professionals and even users are constantly experiencing is at the root of this scourge: "Viruses".

The resulting consequences have been serious.

The effects of this virus are often felt at a time when the need is greatest, for example :

- when staff are paid,
- during accounting calculations,
- at the General Meeting (highlights),
- in short, during influential work for which the applicant is patiently awaiting the outcome, etc.

The requestor does not take into account[1] all the procedures for obtaining answers, thinking that it is the computer that carries out all the operations, whereas it is a great technical exercise for computer specialists to organise the[2] service or the technical application to achieve the objective.

The people behind all these scourges have never often been identified, and until now they have been working underground.

This is why we are making this manual available to everyone, with full veracity at ideas, to help people understand this scourge.

However, the points we make here in this manual, whether they

[1] Mukedi Diesta-Mputu D., Quelques résolutions majeures des difficultés professionnelles en informatique de gestion/entreprise, EUE, 2024 p 56

[2] Mukedi Diesta-Mputu D., L'organisation d'un service informatique dans un système de gestion/entreprise, EUE, 2024 p. 15

are recent or not, are intended to provide guidance and to stimulate your understanding, as we hope they will.

Let this not be a stumbling block, but rather a point of reference for exploring differences.

"The author

General information on viruses

Today's world advocates interests whose thirst for money is unbridled at every level and for every individual, especially the rich. They even want to take the lives of others in order to earn more and earn a lot, while at the same time victimising the most disadvantaged, which is deplorable given that complementarity exists, which in turn advocates equality because no one is enough on their own, ever, ever!

This attitude set out in our book: mental poverty, a nuclear weapon 'rampant', what did we say it's a state of mind, yet everyone needs each other and everyone has the same[3] rights and duties, why so?

Now even the world of information and communication technology has fallen victim to this mental poverty[3] . Viruses".

The virus, which has been relatively widely used in the health/medical sciences, transcended into a computer system and has the same effects as nuclear weapons.

In the health sciences, it is a microbe that is at the root of many of the consequences of human life, and in computing, it systematically or automatically impairs the functioning of a computer system.

The scourge that has ravaged and is ravaging the world today, the fear of which confuses us.

The Democratic Republic of Congo has become a world reference in the health field with the case of the Ebola virus since

[3] Mukedi Diest-Mputu D., La pauvreté mentale, une arme nucléaire "sévissant", EUE, 2024 p.18

1976[4] , which we have all experienced and continue to experience other cases: the coronavirus-2019, at present we are talking about the monkeypox virus. These contagious diseases are exploding and the whole population is on the lookout for them. More seriously, they have serious and fatal consequences, often costing human lives.

When transcended into a computer, it permanently alters the life of an entire computer system.

[4] Lemag.ird.fr,Jean Jacques Muyembe,

CHAPTER I: ORIGIN AND SOME TYPES OF VIRUS

1- Origin

a- Origin of viruses

At least there is another confirmation at this time of year, but in reality, until now, the origin of viruses and harmful programmes has remained obscure, due to the operational clandestinity of their designers/companies, which makes them very difficult to locate and even identify.

Taking into account their after-effects, our experience and the consequences we have lived through, lead us to emphasise that there are relatively two fundamental reasons (objectives) for their origin:

1- Nuisance/destruction: although these designers operate clandestinely, their aim is to harm/destroy the information systems that have been set up to ensure the smooth running of businesses.

2- The Business, acting clandestinely, launching viruses on the market, themselves also manufacture anti-viruses, which they used to test; given that this testing benefited computer scientists and users[5] , they have abolished it, selling them directly for their own immediate gain.

Stymied by the difficulties of getting attacked information systems up and running again, computer specialists or users feel obliged to buy anti-virus software to protect themselves, which enriches the underground, who in turn find themselves well off

---

[5] Idem, p 40

and earning their bread illicitly.

b-Origin of the word virus

The word virus comes from the Latin word for poison[6]

1- A very small infectious agent that has only one type of nucleic acid, DNA or RNA, and can only reproduce by parasitising a cell.

2- Principle of moral contagion, the virus of protest

Poison is a substance that is harmful to all living things: in plants, insects, animals, and especially humans, who are the most fragile. It has various names depending on its purpose or mission, and several types are currently ravaging us according to their targets.

3- In IT

Parasitic instruction or sequence of instructions introduced into a program and liable to cause various disturbances in the operation of the computer.

Today, the consequences are felt wherever IT management is applied without embarrassment, delay or fear. This is causing great panic among company managers, and total insecurity. To resist this, a number of high-quality measures are envisaged, requiring in-depth knowledge to support others in the face of this scourge, which is referred to as IT security, i.e. the security of an information system .[7]

Certainly, an ephemeral breeze will bring relief to the world in question in one way or another, but measures and

[6] Le petit Larousse illustré 2009, p.1070
[7] Wikipedia

recommendations need to be implemented.

A **virus** is a small computer program located in the body of another program, which, when executed, loads itself into memory and executes the instructions that its author has programmed. The definition of a virus could be as follows: "any computer program capable of infecting another computer program by modifying it in such a way that it can in turn reproduce itself".

The real name given to viruses is *CPA* or *Code Auto-Propagable,* but by analogy with the medical field, the name "virus" has been given to them.

2- Type of Virus

Terminate and stay resident (**TSR***)* **viruses** load themselves into the computer's RAM to infect executable files launched by the user. Non-resident viruses infect programs on the hard disk as soon as they are run.

The scope of viruses ranges from the simple ping-pong ball that crosses the screen to the data-destroying virus, the latter being the most dangerous form of virus. So, given that there is a vast range of viruses with actions as diverse as they are varied, viruses are not classified according to their damage but according to their mode of propagation and infection.

There are different types of virus:

- . worms are viruses capable of spreading across a network
- Trojans are viruses used to create a vulnerability in a system (generally to enable the creator to break into the infected system and take control of it).
- . logic bombs are viruses capable of being triggered by a

specific event (system date, remote activation, etc.)

Over the last few years, another phenomenon has appeared: hoaxes, i.e. announcements received by e-mail (for example the announcement of the appearance of a new destructive virus or the possibility of winning a free mobile phone) accompanied by a note telling people to forward the news to all their friends and family. The aim of this process is to clog up the networks and spread disinformation.

Mutant viruses

In reality, most viruses are clones, or more accurately "**mutant viruses**", i.e. viruses that have been rewritten by other users to modify their behaviour or signature.

The fact that there are several versions (known as **variants**) of the same virus makes it all the more difficult to spot, as antivirus publishers have to add these new signatures to their databases.

Polymorphic viruses

Since antivirus software detects viruses by their signature (the succession of bits that identifies them), some virus creators have thought of giving them the ability to automatically change their appearance, like a chameleon, by equipping viruses with functions for encrypting and decrypting their signature, so that only these viruses are able to recognise their own signature. This type of virus is known as a "**polymorphic virus**" (a word derived from the Greek meaning *"which can take several forms").*

Retroviruses

A "**retrovirus**" or "*bounty hunter* virus" is a virus with the ability to modify anti-virus signatures to render them inoperative.

Boot sector viruses

A "**boot sector virus**" is a virus capable of infecting a hard disk's boot sector *(MBR,* or *master boot record), i*.e. a sector of the disk copied into memory when the computer starts up, then executed to boot the operating system.

Trans-applicative viruses (macro viruses)

With the proliferation of programs using macros, Microsoft has developed a common scripting language that can be inserted into most documents containing macros: VBScript, a subset of Visual Basic. These viruses are now able to infect macros in Microsoft Office documents, meaning that such a virus can be located inside an ordinary Word or Excel document, and execute a portion of the code when the document is opened, enabling it not only to spread through the files, but also to access the operating system (usually Windows).

However, an increasing number of applications support Visual Basic, so these viruses are conceivable in many other applications that support VBScript.

The beginning of the third millennium saw the widespread appearance of Visual Basic scripts distributed by e-mail as attachments (identifiable by their *.VBS* extension*)* with an e-mail title urging the user to open the poisoned gift.

When opened in a Microsoft email client, it can access the entire address book and self-distribute over the network. This type of virus is known as a worm.

Current worms

Today's worms are spread mainly via email (and in particular the

Outlook email client) by means of attached files containing instructions for retrieving all the email addresses contained in the address book and sending copies of themselves to all these recipients.

These worms are usually scripts (usually VBScript) or executable files sent as attachments and triggered when the recipient user clicks on the attached file.

CHAPTER 2: SOME PROTECTIVE MEASURES

Let's put it this way: certain measures are taken to combat viruses - let's talk about the software/programmes designed, known as anti-viruses.

Some more flexible and dynamic operating systems are resisting this scourge: the Unix family (Ubuntu, Unix, Lunix) and some of the more advanced versions of Windows too.

These same anti-viruses have set time limits for their use, and once they have expired, they too become viruses.

Anti-virus concept

An anti-virus is a programme capable of detecting the presence of viruses on a computer and, where possible, disinfecting it. The procedure for cleaning a computer is known as virus eradication.

There are several eradication methods:

- Deleting the code corresponding to the virus from the infected file ;
- Deleting the infected file ;
- Quarantining the infected file, by moving it to a location where it cannot be executed.

1- Virus detection

Viruses reproduce by infecting *"host applications", i.*e. by copying a portion of executable code within an existing program. To avoid chaotic operation, viruses are programmed not to infect the same file several times. They therefore include in the infected application a sequence of bytes enabling them to check whether the programme has already been infected: this is the viral signature.

Antivirus software relies on this signature, which is specific to each virus, to detect them. This is the **signature search** method *(scanning),* the oldest method used by anti-virus software. This method is only reliable if the anti-virus has an up-to-date virus database, i.e. one containing the signatures of all known viruses. However, this method does not allow the detection of viruses that have not yet been listed by anti-virus publishers. What's more, virus programmers have now endowed them with camouflage capabilities, so as to make their signature difficult to detect, or even undetectable; these are known as "**polymorphic viruses**".

Some antivirus programs use an **integrity checker** to check whether files have been modified. The integrity checker builds a database containing information about executable files on the system (modification date, size, and possibly a checksum). When an executable file changes its characteristics, the antivirus warns the user of the machine.

2- Protection

Protecting yourself from a worm infection is simple. The best method is not to "blindly" open files sent to you as attachments.

This means that all files that can be executed or interpreted by the operating system can potentially infect your computer. Files with the following extensions in particular are potentially susceptible to infection:

exe, com, bat, pif, vbs, scr, doc, xls, msi, eml

Under Windows, it is advisable to deactivate the *"hide*

extensions" function, as this can mislead the user as to the true extension of a file. For example, a file with the extension *.jpg.vbs* will appear as a file with the extension *.jpg*!

Files with the following extensions are not interpreted by the system and therefore present a minimal risk of infection:

txt, jpg, gif, bmp, avi, mpg, asf, dat, mp3,

wav, mid, ram, rm

It is often said that GIF or JPG files may contain viruses.

Any file can contain a piece of computer code carrying a virus, but the system will need to have been modified by another virus before it can interpret the code contained in these files!

For all files whose extension might suggest that the file is infected (or for extensions you don't know), don't hesitate to install an antivirus and systematically scan the attached file before opening it.

Here is a more complete (non-exhaustive) list of file extensions likely to be infected by a :

Extensions

386, ACE, ACM, ACV, ARC, ARJ, ASD, ASP, AVB, AX, BAT, BIN, BOO, BTM, CAB, CLA, CLASS, CDR, CHM, CMD, CNV, COM, CPL, CPT, CSC, CSS, DLL, DOC, DOT DRV, DVB, DWG, EML, EXE, FON, GMS, GVB, HLP, HTA, HTM, HTML, HTA, HTT, INF, INI, JS, JSE, LNK, MDB, MHT, MHTM, MHTML, MPD, MPP, MPT, MSG, MSI, MSO, NWS, OBD, OBJ, OBT, OBZ, OCX, OFT, OV?, PCI, PIF, PL, PPT, PWZ, POT, PRC, QPW, RAR, SCR, SBF, SH, SHB, SHS, SHTML, SHW, SMM, SYS, TAR.GZ, TD0, TGZ, TT6, TLB, TSK, TSP, VBE, VBS, VBX, VOM, VS? VWP, VXE, VXD, WBK, WBT, WIZ, WK?, WPC, WPD, WML, WSH, WSC, XML, XLS, XLT, ZIP

Nowadays, with the significant advances in computer hardware and the widespread use of the Internet, setting the operating system to download is also one of the ways of combating this technical scourge.

Avoid access to all external media, i.e. mass storage from non-insurance third parties.

Copies in several other machines can also help in this respect.

The back-up of all the company's sensitive[8] programmes protects against corrosive attacks.

[8] Mukedi Diesta-Mputu D., the Organisation of page 13

CHAPTER 3: THE TROJAN HORSE AND ITS MEANDERS

Trojan horse[9]

A **Trojan** *horse* is a computer programme that carries out malicious operations without the user's knowledge. The name "Trojan Horse" comes from a legend told in the *Iliad* (by the writer *Homer)* about the siege of the city of Troy by the Greeks.

In computing, a Trojan horse is a program hidden inside another program that executes commands surreptitiously, and generally gives access to the machine on which it is executed by opening a **backdoor**. By extension, it is sometimes called a **Trojan** by analogy with the inhabitants of the city of Troy.

Like a virus, a Trojan horse is a harmful code (programme) placed inside a healthy programme (imagine a fake file listing command that destroys files instead of displaying a list).

A Trojan horse can, for example

- . stealing passwords ;
- . copy sensitive data ;
- . perform any other harmful action ;
- . etc.

Worse still, such a program can create a deliberate security breach from inside your network, allowing access to protected parts of the network to people connecting from the outside.

The main Trojan horses are programs that open machine ports,

[9] François P, Encyclopédie Informatique Comment ça marche 2009

i.e. allowing their creator to enter your machine via the network by opening a **backdoor**. This is why they are generally referred to as *backdoors* or *backorifices*.

A Trojan horse is not necessarily a virus, since its purpose is not to reproduce itself and infect other machines. On the other hand, some viruses can also be Trojan horses, i.e. propagate like a virus and open a port on infected machines!

Detecting such a programme is difficult because it is necessary to detect whether or not the action of the programme (the Trojan horse) is intended by the user.

1- Symptoms of infection

Infection by a Trojan horse generally follows the opening of a contaminated file containing the Trojan horse (see the article on protection against worms) and results in the following symptoms:

- . abnormal modem or network card activity: data is loaded when there is no user activity ;
- . curious reactions from mice ;
- . impromptu programme openings ;
- . repeated crashes ;

2- The Trojan horse principle

The principle behind Trojan horses is generally (and increasingly) to open a port on your machine to allow a hacker to take control of it (for example to steal personal data stored on the disk). The hacker's aim is firstly to infect your machine by getting you to open an infected file containing the Trojan, and secondly to access your machine via the port he has opened.

However, in order to infiltrate your machine, the hacker generally needs to know its IP address. So :

- . or you have a fixed IP address (in the case of a company or sometimes private individuals connected by cable, etc.), from which the IP address can be easily retrieved.
- . or your IP address is dynamic (assigned to each connection), as is the case for modem connections, in which case the hacker must scan IP addresses at random to detect IP addresses corresponding to infected machines.

3- The fight against the Trojans

To protect yourself from this kind of intrusion, simply install a firewall, i.e. a programme that filters communications entering and leaving your machine. A *firewall* allows you to see communications leaving your machine (normally initiated by programs you use) or incoming communications. However, it is possible for the firewall to detect connections from the outside world without you being the **chosen victim of** a hacker. This may be due to tests carried out by your ISP or a hacker scanning a range of IP addresses at random.

For Windows-based systems, there are some very powerful free firewalls:

- . ZoneAlarm
- . Tiny personal firewall

4- Infection

If a program of unknown origin tries to open a connection, the firewall will ask you for confirmation before initiating the connection. It is essential not to authorise connections to programmes you don't know, as they could very well be Trojan horses.

In the event of a recurrence, it may be useful to check that your computer is not infected by a Trojan by using a programme to detect and eliminate them (known as a *Trojan horse).*

List of ports usually used by Trojans

Trojans usually open a port on the infected machine and wait for a connection to be opened on that port before giving full control to potential hackers. Here is a (non-exhaustive) list of the main ports used by Trojan horses (source: Rico website):

Port	Trojan
21	Back construction, Blade runner, Doly, Fore, FTP trojan, Invisible FTP, Larva, WebEx, WinCrash
23	TTS (Tiny Telnet Server)
25	Ajan, Antigen, Email Password Sender, Happy99, Kuang 2, ProMail trojan, Shtrilitz, Stealth, Tapiras, Terminator, WinPC, WinSpy
31	Agent 31, Hackers Paradise, Masters Paradise
41	Deep Throat
59	DMSetup
79	FireHotcker
80	Executor, RingZero
99	Hidden port
110	ProMail trojan
113	Kazimas
119	Happy 99
121	JammerKillah
421	TCP Wrappers
456	Hackers Paradise
531	Rasmin
555	Ini-Killer, NetAdmin, Phase Zero, Stealth Spy
666	Attack FTP, Back Construction, Cain & Abel, Satanz Backdoor, ServeU, Shadow Phyre
911	Dark Shadow
999	Deep Throat, WinSatan
1002	Silencer, WebEx
1010 à 1015	Doly trojan

1024	NetSpy
1042	Bla
1045	Rasmin
1090	Xtreme
1170	Psyber Stream Server, Streaming Audio Trojan, voice
1234	Ultor trojan
port 1234	Ultors Trojan
port 1243	BackDoor-G, SubSeven, SubSeven Apocalypse
port 1245	VooDoo Doll
port 1269	Mavericks Matrix
port 1349 (UDP)	BO DLL
port 1492	FTP99CMP
port 1509	Psyber Streaming Server
port 1600	Shivka-Burka
port 1807	SpySender
port 1981	Shockrave
port 1999	BackDoor
port 1999	TransScout
port 2000	TransScout
port 2001	TransScout
port 2001	Trojan Cow
port 2002	TransScout
port 2003	TransScout
port 2004	TransScout
port 2005	TransScout
port 2023	Ripper
port 2115	Bugs
port 2140	Deep Throat, The Invasor

port 2155	Illusion Mailer
port 2283	HVL Rat5
port 2565	Striker
port 2583	WinCrash
port 2600	Digital RootBeer
port 2801	Phineas Phucker
Port 2989(UDP)	RAT
port 3024	WinCrash
port 3128	RingZero
port 3129	Masters Paradise
port 3150	Deep Throat, The Invasor
port 3459	Eclipse 2000
port 3700	portal of Doom
port 3791	Eclypse
port 3801 (UDP)	Eclypse
port 4092	WinCrash
port 4321	BoBo
port 4567	File Nail
port 4590	ICQTrojan
port 5000	Bubbel, Back Door Setup, Trojan Sockets
port 5001	Back Door Setup, Trojan Sockets
port 5011	One of the Last Trojans (OOTLT)
port 5031	NetMetro
port 5321	Firehotcker
port 5400	Blade Runner, Back Construction
port 5401	Blade Runner, Back Construction
port 5402	Blade Runner, Back Construction
port 5550	Xtcp
port 5512	Illusion Mailer

port 5555	ServeMe
port 5556	BO Facil
port 5557	BO Facil
port 5569	Robo-Hack
port 5742	WinCrash
port 6400	The Thing
port 6669	Vampyre
port 6670	DeepThroat
port 6771	DeepThroat
port 6776	BackDoor-G, SubSeven
port 6912	Shit Heep (not port 69123!)
port 6939	Indoctrination
port 6969	GateCrasher, Priority, IRC 3
port 6970	GateCrasher
port 7000	Remote Grab, Kazimas
port 7300	NetMonitor
port 7301	NetMonitor
port 7306	NetMonitor
port 7307	NetMonitor
port 7308	NetMonitor
port 7789	Back Door Setup, ICKiller
port 8080	RingZero
port 9400	InCommand
port 9872	portal of Doom
port 9873	portal of Doom
port 9874	portal of Doom
port 9875	portal of Doom
port 9876	Cyber Attacker
port 9878	TransScout
port 9989	iNi-Killer

port 10067 (UDP)	portal of Doom
port 10101	BrainSpy
port 10167 (UDP)	portal of Doom
port 10520	Acid Shivers
port 10607	Coma
port 11000	Senna Spy
port 11223	Progenic trojan
port 12076	Gjamer
port 12223	Hack'99 KeyLogger
port 12345	GabanBus, NetBus, Pie Bill Gates, X-bill
port 12346	GabanBus, NetBus, X-bill
port 12361	Whack-a-mole
port 12362	Whack-a-mole
port 12631	WhackJob
port 13000	Senna Spy
port 16969	Priority
port 17300	Kuang2 The Virus
port 20000	Millennium
port 20001	Millennium
port 20034	NetBus 2 Pro
port 20203	Logged
port 21544	GirlFriend
port 22222	Prosiak
port 23456	Evil FTP, Ugly FTP, Whack Job
port 23476	Donald Dick
port 23477	Donald Dick
port 26274 (UDP)	Delta Source
port 27374	SubSeven 2.0
port 29891 (UDP)	The Unexplained

port 30029	AOL Trojan
port 30100	NetSphere
port 30101	NetSphere
port 30102	NetSphere
port 30303	Trojan sockets
port 30999	Kuang2
port 31336	Bo Whack
port 31337	Baron Night, BO client, BO2, Bo Facil
port 31337 (UDP)	BackFire, Back Orifice, DeepBO
port 31338	NetSpy DK
port 31338 (UDP)	Back Orifice, DeepBO
port 31339	NetSpy DK
port 31666	BOWhack
port 31785	Hack'a'Tack
port 31787	Hack'a'Tack
port 31788	Hack'a'Tack
port 31789 (UDP)	Hack'a'Tack
port 31791 (UDP)	Hack'a'Tack
port 31792	Hack'a'Tack
port 33333	Prosiak
port 33911	Spirit 2001a
port 34324	BigGluck, TN
port 40412	The Spy
port 40421	Agent 40421, Masters Paradise
port 40422	Masters Paradise
port 40423	Masters Paradise
port 40426	Masters Paradise
port 47262 (UDP)	Delta Source
port 50505	Trojan sockets
port 50766	Fore, Schwindler
port 53001	Remote Windows Shutdown
port 54320	Back Orifice 2000
port 54321	School Bus

port 54321 (UDP)	Back Orifice 2000
port 60000	Deep Throat
port 61466	Telecommando
port 65000	Devil

CHAPTER 4: SOME HARMFUL FEATURES OF COMPUTER NETWORKS

1- Logic bombs

Logic bombs are programmed devices which are triggered at a specific time by exploiting the system date, the launch of a command, or any call to the system.

This type of virus is capable of activating at a precise moment on a large number of machines (known as a *time bomb).*

Logic bombs are generally used to create a denial of service by saturating the network connections of a site, online service or company.

2- Spyware

Spyware is a programme that collects information about the user of the computer on which it is installed (sometimes referred to as *a spy)* and sends it to the company that distributes it, enabling it to draw up a profile of Internet users (known as *profiling).*

The information gathered can be :

- . traceability of URLs of sites visited,
- . tracking keywords entered into search engines,
- . analysis of internet purchases,
- . or even bank payment details (credit card / VISA number)
- . or personal information.

Spyware is generally installed at the same time as other software (usually freeware or shareware). This enables the authors of such software to make a profit from selling statistical information, and thus distribute their software free of charge. This is a business model in which free software is obtained in exchange for the transfer of personal data.

Spyware is not necessarily illegal because the user licence for the software it comes with specifies that this third-party programme will be installed! However, as users rarely read the full user licence, they are rarely aware that such software is profiling them behind their backs.

In addition to the damage caused by the disclosure of personal information, spyware can also be a source of various other nuisances:

- RAM consumption,
- use of disk space,
- mobilising processor resources,
- other applications crash,
- ergonomic inconvenience (for example, the opening of advertising screens targeted according to the data collected).

3- Types of spyware

There are generally two types of spyware:

- **Internal spyware** (or *internal spyware* or *integrated spyware)* with direct lines of code dedicated to data collection functions.

- **External spyware**, autonomous collection programs installed Here is a non-exhaustive list of non-integrated spyware :

Alexa, Aureate/Radiate, BargainBuddy, ClickTillUWin, Conducent Timesink, Cydoor, Comet Cursor, Doubleclick, DSSAgent, EverAd, eZula/KaZaa Toptext, Flashpoint/ Flashtrack, Flyswat, Gator/Claria, GoHip, Hotbar, ISTbar, Lop, NewDotNet, Realplayer, SaveNow, Songspy, Xupiter, Web3000 and WebHancer

Protecting yourself

The main difficulty with spyware is detecting it. The best way to protect yourself is not to install any software if you are not 100% sure of its origin and reliability (particularly freeware, shareware and peer-to-peer file exchange software). Here are a few examples (not an exhaustive list) of software known to contain one or more spyware programs: Babylon Translator, GetRight, Go!Zilla, Download Accelerator, Cute FTP, PKZip, KaZaA and iMesh.

What's more, uninstalling this type of software rarely removes the spyware that accompanies it. Worse still, it can cause other applications to malfunction!

In practice, it is almost impossible not to install software. The presence of suspicious background processes, strange files or worrying entries in the registry can sometimes betray the presence of spyware in the system.

If you don't go through your registry with a fine-toothed comb every day, rest assured that there is **anti-spyware** software available to detect and remove files, processes and registry entries created by spyware.

Installing a personal firewall can also detect the presence of spyware and prevent it from accessing the Internet (and transmitting the information it collects).

4- Some anti-spyware products

The best-known and most effective anti-spyware products include :

Ad-Aware from Lavasoft.de Spybot Search&Destroy

Keyloggers

A **keylogger** is a device that records keystrokes and saves them without the user's knowledge. It is therefore a spying device.

Some keyloggers are able to record URLs visited, e-mails consulted or sent, files opened, and even create a video of all computer activity!

As keyloggers record all keystrokes, they can be used by malicious people to recover the passwords of workstation users! This means that you need to be particularly vigilant when using a computer you can't trust (such as an open-access workstation in a company, school or public place like an Internet café).

5- Keyloggers: software or hardware

Keyloggers can be either software or hardware. The former involves a stealth process (or one with a name closely resembling the name of a system process), writing the captured information to a hidden file! Keyloggers can also be hardware: a device (cable or dongle) inserted between the computer's keyboard socket and the keyboard.

Protecting yourself from keyloggers

The best way to protect yourself is to be vigilant:

- . Do not install software of dubious origin,
- . Be careful when you log on to a computer that does not belong to you! If it's an open-access computer, take a quick look at the configuration before logging on to sites that ask for your password, to see if other users have been there before you and whether or not it's possible for an ordinary user to install software. If in doubt, do not connect to secure sites where there is a risk (online banking, etc.).

If you have the opportunity, inspect the computer with anti-spyware software.

Presentation of the Sircam virus

The Sircam virus (codename *W32.Sircam.Worm@mm, Backdoor.SirCam* or *Troj_Sircam.a)* is an e-mail-spreading worm. It particularly affects Microsoft Outlook users on Windows 95, 98, Millenium and 2000 operating systems.

The actions of the virus

The Sircam worm randomly selects a document (with extension *.gif, .jpg, .mpg, .jpeg, .mpeg, .mov, .pdf, .png, .ps or .zip) located in the c:My Documents* directory *of* the infected computer, then automatically sends an e-mail with the name of this document as the subject, the body of which is one of the following two messages:

. In English

."Hi! How are you?

. I send you this file in order to have your advice See you later. Thanks"

"Hi! How are you?

I hope you can help me with this file that I send

See you later. Thanks"

"Hi! How are you?

I hope you like the file that I send to you

See you later. Thanks"

. Or in Spanish

. "Hola como estas?

. Te mando este archivo para que me des tu punto de vista Nos vemos pronto, gracias."

The Sircam virus attaches a copy of itself to the message, the name of which is that of the file retrieved from the user's disk with the double extension *.vbs.*

The Sircam worm also runs the risk of deleting all the files on your hard disk on 16 October each year if your computer uses a European date format (day/month/year).

Sircam also adds text to the *c:\recycled\sircam.sys* file each time the machine is rebooted, which potentially saturates the space available on the *C:* drive.

Symptoms of infection

Infected machines have :

. Sirc32.exe

. Sircam.sys

. Run32.exe

To check whether you are infected, search all your hard disks for the files listed above *(Start/Search/Files or Folders).*

CHAPTER 5: SOME ERADICATION PROCEDURES.

These are procedures or methods that can provide relief from the harmful effects of viruses on an attacked system, and vary from one virus to another.

1- For the virus

The best way to eradicate the Sircam worm is to use a recent antivirus or the disinfection kit from Symantec :

You can also carry out a manual disinfection by following the procedure below:

- Delete the files *Sirc32.exe* and *Sircam.sys*
- Delete the file *c:\windows\Runddl32.exe*
- Rename the file *c:\windows\Run32.exe* to *c:\windows\Rundll32.exe*

Introducing the Magist virus

The Magistr virus (codename *W32/Magistr.b@MM, I-Worm.Magistr.b.poly* or *PE_MAGISTR.B)* is a polymorphic worm (i.e. a worm whose form, or more precisely signature, changes continuously) that spreads via e-mail. It is a variant of the *Disemboweler* worm *(Magistr.A),* particularly affecting users of Microsoft Outlook, Eudora or Netscape e-mail clients running Windows 95, 98, Millenium and 2000 operating systems.

2- The actions of the virus

The Magistr.B virus searches the address book files on the system (respectively with extensions .WAB and .DBX/.MBX for

Outlook and Eudora clients), in order to select the recipients of the message.

The subject and body of the message sent by the Magistr worm are chosen at random from a file extract found on the disk of the infected computer.

The Magistr virus attaches a copy of itself to the message, the name of which contains an extension (or double extension) such as *.com, .bat, .pif, .exe or .vbs.*

The Magistr worm also risks deleting all the information contained in :

- CMOS
- the BIOS
- The hard disk

The Magistr.B virus can seriously damage your system and the information stored on it.

In addition, the Magistr.B virus is able to disable the *ZoneAlarm* personal firewall using the *WM_QUIT* command.

Symptoms of infection

Infected machines have the following characteristics:

Moving the mouse pointer over the desktop moves the icons.

1- For the Magistr virus

The best method is to use a recent antivirus or disinfection kit.

Presentation of the Nimda virus

The Nimda virus (codename *W32/Nimda*) is a worm that spreads via e-mail, but it also exploits 4 other propagation methods:

- . The web
- . Shared directories
- . Microsoft IIS server vulnerabilities
- . File exchanges

The actions of the virus

The Nimda worm retrieves the list of addresses in the address books of Microsoft Outlook and Eudora, as well as the e-mail addresses contained in HTML files on the disk of the infected machine.

The Nimda virus then sends all recipients an email with an empty body, a random and often very long subject and attaches an attachment named *Readme.exe* or *Readme.eml* (file encapsulating an executable file). Viruses using an *.eml* extension exploit a flaw in Microsoft Internet Explorer 5.

The Nimda virus is also capable of spreading through shared directories on Microsoft Windows networks by infecting executable files located there.

Viewing web pages on servers infected with the Nimda virus can lead to infection when a user views these pages with a vulnerable Microsoft Internet Explorer 5 browser.

The Nimda virus is also capable of taking control of a Microsoft IIS (Internet Information Server) web server by exploiting certain security flaws.

Finally, the virus infects executable files on the infected machine, which means that it is also capable of spreading by file exchange.

Symptoms of infection

Workstations infected with the Nimda worm have the following files on their disk:

- README.EXE
- README.EML
- files with the .NWS extension
- files with names like *mep*.tmp, mep*.tmp.exe* (for example *mepE002.tmp.exe)*

To check whether you are infected, search all your hard disks for the files listed above *(Start/Search/Files or Folders).*

2- For the Nimda virus

The best method is to first disconnect the infected machine from the network, then use a recent antivirus or the disinfection kit offered by Symantec:

In addition, the virus is spread via a security flaw in Microsoft Internet Explorer, which means that you can be infected by the virus by browsing an infected site. To remedy this, you need to download the patch (software fix) for Microsoft Internet Explorer 5.01 and 5.5. Please check your browser version and download the patch if necessary: http://www.microsoft.com/windows/ie/download/critical/Q290108/de fault.asp

Presentation of the BadTrans virus

The BadTrans virus (codename *W32.BadTrans.B* or *W32/Badtrans-B)* is an e-mail-spreading worm. It also exploits another propagation method:

- . Microsoft Internet Explorer vulnerabilities

The BadTrans.B virus particularly affects Microsoft Outlook users running Windows 95, 98, Millenium, NT4 and 2000 operating systems, as the virus is activated simply by viewing the message (i.e. even if the user does not click on the attachment). http://www.microsoft.com/technet/security/bulletin/MS01-020.asp **Virus actions**

The BadTrans worm retrieves the list of addresses present in the address books of the infected user, as well as web pages contained in Internet cache folders and in the *My Documents* directory.

Then the BadTrans virus sends all recipients a :

- . with an empty body, or with the phrase *Take a look to the attachment.*
- . with subject *Re: <Found mail subject>.*
- . whose attachment has a name consisting of three parts

o Part I: one of the following texts :

  - CARD
  - DOCS
  - FUN
  - HAMSTER NEWS_DOC

- HUMOR
- IMAGES
- ME_NUDE
- New_Napster_Site
- News_doc
- PICS
- README
- S3MSONG
- SEARCHURL
- SETUP
- Sorry_about_yesterday
- YOU_ARE_FAT!

- Second part: one of the following extensions:
  - .DOC
  - .MP3
  - .ZIP
- Third and final part: one of the following extensions:
  - .pif
  - .scr

The message will contain an attachment of the type :

. Me_Nude.MP3.scr

- News_doc.DOC.scr
- HAMSTER.DOC.pif
- PICS.doc.scr
- HUMOR.MP3.scr
- README.MP3.scr
- FUN.MP3.pif
- YOU_are_FAT!.MP3.scr
- ...

Symptoms of infection

Workstations infected with the BadTrans worm have the following file on their disk:

- kdll.dll, a Trojan horse that can record keystrokes to recover your data.

password

To check whether you are infected, search all your hard disks for the files listed above *(Start/Search/Files or Folders).*

3- For the BadTrans virus

The best way to eradicate the BadTrans worm is first to disconnect the infected machine from the network, and then to use a recent anti-virus software.

In addition, the virus spreads via a security flaw in Microsoft Outlook, which means that you can be infected by the virus without clicking on the attachment. To remedy this, you need to download the patch (software fix) for Microsoft Outlook. Please check your email client and download the patch if necessary: http://www.microsoft.com/technet/security/bulletin/MS01-020.asp **Klez virus overview**

The Klez virus appeared in early 2002 and is now omnipresent on networks. The risk it represents is all the greater now that new variants of the virus are constantly appearing (Klez.e, Klez.g, Klez.h, Klez.i, Klez.k, etc.). The new versions of the virus incorporate increasingly innovative distribution mechanisms, making it easier and easier to spread. The KLEZ virus (codename *W32.Klez.Worm@mm) is* a worm that spreads via e-mail. It also exploits 4 other propagation methods:

- . The web
- . Shared directories
- . Microsoft IIS server vulnerabilities
- . File exchanges

It particularly affects users of Microsoft Outlook on Windows 95, 98, Millenium, NT4, 2000 and XP operating systems, as well as users of Microsoft Internet Explorer.

The actions of the virus

The Klez worm retrieves the list of addresses in the address books of Microsoft Outlook, Eudora and instant messaging software (ICQ).

The Klez virus then sends mail to all recipients using its own SMTP server.

The Klez virus, for example, is capable of generating emails with an empty body and a subject randomly chosen from a range of around a hundred predefined themes, and attaches an executable attachment containing a variant of the virus. Viruses using an *.eml* extension exploit a flaw in Microsoft Internet Explorer 5.

A particular feature of the Klez virus is its ability to send emails pretending to be from a sender whose address has been found on the victim's machine (the virus tampers with the *from* field of the email sent).

The most recent variants of the virus even include tools that enable them to render the main anti-virus software obsolete.

To add insult to injury, the authors of the virus have programmed it to send victims a pseudo-corrective against itself in an e-mail entitled *Worm Klez.E immunity.* The mail also sends fake error messages indicating that a message could not be delivered, and once again containing a copy of the virus as an attachment!

The Klez virus is also capable of spreading through shared directories on Microsoft Windows networks by infecting executable files located there.

Viewing web pages on servers infected with the Klez virus can lead to infection when a user views these pages with a vulnerable Microsoft Internet Explorer 5 browser.

The Nimda virus is also capable of taking control of a Microsoft IIS (Internet Information Server) web server by exploiting certain security flaws.

Finally, like its brethren, the virus infects executable files on the infected machine, which means that it is also capable of spreading by file exchange.

To complete the picture, the Klez virus is scheduled to delete randomly selected files every sixth day (i.e. the 6th of the month) of odd-numbered months. The icing on the cake: on 6 January and 6 July the virus deletes all the files on the disk!

Symptoms of infection

The Klez virus uses as many resources as possible on the infected machine. If your computer reacts slowly and strangely, the first thing to do is to scan all your disks with your antivirus, bearing in mind that the virus may have modified the antivirus to avoid detection...

4- For the Klez virus

To eradicate the Klez worm, the best method is to first disconnect the infected machine from the network, then use a recent antivirus or the disinfection kit offered by Symantec (preferably restarting the computer in safe mode):

Download the disinfection kit

In addition, the virus is spread via a security flaw in Microsoft Internet Explorer, which means that you can be infected by the virus by browsing an infected site. To remedy this, you need to download the patch (software fix) for Microsoft Internet Explorer 5.01 and 5.5. Please check your browser version and download the patch if necessary: http://www.microsoft.com/windows/ie/download/critical/Q290108/de fault.asp

As the virus falsifies the sender's email address (*from* field), we advise you not to reply to the sender of the virus but to look at the *Return-Path* field of the email and write a message to the sender!

More information on the virus

- . http://solutions.journaldunet.com/0204/020419_klez.shtml
- . http://vil.nai.com/vil/content/v_99367.htm
- . http://www.antivirus.com/vinfo/virusencyclo/default5.asp?VName=WORM_KLEZ.E
- . http://www.01net.com/rdn?oid=178276
- . http://securityresponse.symantec.com/avcenter/venc/data/w32.klez.h@mm.html

http://www.kav.ch/avpve/worms/email/klez.stm **Presentation of the LovSan virus**

The LovSan virus (also known as *W32/Lovsan.worm, W32/Lovsan.worm.b, W32.Blaster.Worm, W32/Blaster-B, WORM_MSBLAST.A, MSBLASTER, Win32.Poza, Win32.Posa.Worm, Win32.Poza.B)* is the first virus to exploit the RPC/DCOM *(Remote Procedure Call)* flaw in Microsoft Windows systems, enabling remote processes to communicate. By exploiting the flaw via a buffer overflow, a malicious program (such as the LovSan virus) can take control of the vulnerable machine.

The actions of the virus

The **LovSan / Blaster** worm is programmed to scan a random range of IP addresses for systems vulnerable to the RPC flaw on port 135.

When a vulnerable machine is found, the worm opens a remote shell on TCP port 4444, and forces the remote machine to download a copy of the worm to the *%o WinDir%o\system32* directory by running a *TFTP* command (port 69 UDP) to transfer the file from the infected machine.

Once the file has been downloaded, it is executed and then creates entries in the registry so that it restarts automatically each time the system is rebooted:

- HKEY_LOCAL_MACHINE\SOFTWARE\Microsoft\ Windows\CurrentVersion\
- Run "windows auto update" = msblast.exe I just want to say LOVE YOU SAN!!! bill

To complete the picture, the LovSan/Blaster virus is designed to carry out an attack on Microsoft's *WindowsUpdate* service in order to disrupt the updating of vulnerable machines!

Symptoms of infection

Exploitation of the RPC vulnerability causes a number of malfunctions on affected systems, linked to the disabling of the RPC service (*svchost.exe / rpcss.exe* process). Vulnerable systems present the following symptoms:

- Copy/Paste faulty or impossible
- Hyperlink cannot be opened in a new window
- Unable to move icons
- erratic windows file search function
- closing port 135/TCP

5- *To eradicate the LovSan worm*

The best method is to first disinfect the system using the following disinfection kit: Download the disinfection kit.

Furthermore, as the virus spreads via the Microsoft Windows network, we strongly advise you to install a personal firewall on your machines connected to the Internet and to filter the tcp/69, tcp/135 to tcp/139 and tcp/4444 ports.

More information on the virus

- . Nai
- .Microsoft
- . Sophos
- . Symantec
- Symantec-disinfection tool

Presentation of the Sasser virus

The **Sasser** virus (also known as *W32/Sasser.worm, W32.Sasser.Worm, Worm.Win32.Sasser.a, Worm.Win32.Sasser.b* or *Win32.Sasser)* appeared in May 2004, exploiting a vulnerability in the Windows LSASS *(Local Security Authority Subsystem Service,* corresponding to the lsass.exe executable). The first virus to exploit the flaw in the Windows LSASS service appeared barely two weeks after the flaw was published and the first patches made available.

The actions of the virus

The **Sasser** worm is programmed to launch 128 processes (1024 in the case of the SasserC variant) responsible for scanning a random range of IP addresses for systems vulnerable to the

LSASS flaw on port 445/TCP.

The virus installs an FTP server on port 5554 to make itself available for download to other infected computers,

Then, when a vulnerable machine is found, the worm opens a remote shell on the machine (on TCP port 9996), and forces the remote machine to download a copy of the worm (named *avserve.exe* or *avserve2.exe* for the Sasser.B variant) into the Windows directory.

Once the file has been downloaded, it creates a file called *win.log* (or *win2.log* for the Sasser.B variant) in the *c:*[3] directory to record the number of machines it manages to infect. It then creates entries in the registry to automatically restart itself on each reboot:

- HKLM\Software\Microsoft\Windows\CurrentVersio n\Run\avserve = avserve.exe or

HKLM\Software\Microsoft\Windows\CurrentVersion\Run avserve.exe -> C:\%WINDIR%\avserve.exe

The virus calls the *"AbortSystemShutdown"* function to prevent it from being restarted (or disabled) by the user or by other viruses,

Symptoms of infection

Exploitation of the LSASS vulnerability causes a number of malfunctions on affected systems, linked to the stopping of the LSASS service (*lsass.exe* process*)*. Vulnerable systems present the following symptoms:

.Untimely restarts, the system displays the following message :

.System shutdown initiated by Authority/System

.The system process:

C: \WI ND OWS\system32\lsass.exe

ended unexpectedly with status code 128

.Network traffic on TCP ports 445, 5554 and 9996,

. abrupt shutdown of 'LSASS.EXE' with an error window displaying: lsass.exe-application error

6- To eradicate the virus

The best method is first and foremost to protect the system by activating the firewall.

Then right-click on the Internet connection and click *Properties.* Select the *"Advanced settings"* tab*,* then tick the *"Protect my computer and the network by limiting or prohibiting access to this computer from the Internet"* box *and* confirm by clicking *OK.*

It is then essential to update the system using the Windows Update service or by updating your system with the next patch corresponding to your operating system.

In addition, as the virus spreads via the network, we strongly advise you to install a personal firewall on your machines connected to the Internet and to filter tcp ports.

More information on the virus

- Nai
- F-Secure
- Microsoft
- Sophos
- Symantec
- Symantec-Disinfection tool
- Secuser (Sasser)
- Secuser (LSASS flaw)

What is a disinfection kit?

A disinfection kit is a small executable designed to clean a machine infected by a particular virus. Each disinfection kit is therefore only capable of eradicating a particular type of virus, or even a particular version of a virus.

The disinfection utilities presented below in no way replace the action of antivirus software. Antivirus software plays a preventive role, intercepting the virus before the machine is infected. However, in the event of infection, the disinfection kits you can download from this site will enable you to take corrective measures to eradicate the virus!

How do I use the disinfection utilities?

To eradicate a virus from your machine, as long as you know which virus has infected your system, the best method is to first disconnect the infected machine from the network, and then retrieve the adhoc disinfection kit.

Then restart the computer in safe mode (except for WindowsNT) and run the disinfection utility.

In addition, some worms are spreading via a security flaw in Microsoft Internet

Explorer, which means that you can be infected by the virus by browsing an infected site. To remedy this, download the patch for *Microsoft Internet Explorer.*

CONCLUSION

In short, viruses are software designed to interfere with the genuine operation of computers via their programmes. This is a mechanism that should be condemned, but which meets commercial criteria, i.e. it calls on the operator to buy back the programmes.

We have at least outlined their meanderings and some of the measures of their fight.

Science is complementary, and each of us can make our own contribution to the edifice of knowledge, at least to open up horizons in the grey areas.

For us, this was a major concern, which is why we decided to add a few lines so that all readers could feel at ease in their scientific exercise.

The data provided to scientists comes from both sides, and this competition enhances the content of the book.

If you have any criticisms or suggestions, our arms are always open, because "he who loves science, loves correction".

I'd like to take my hat off to anyone who can continue in the same vein as us: publishing, criticising, encouraging/congratulating and, above all, supporting us financially.

BIBLIOGRAPHY

Publications

1- How it works 2009

2- François, Encyclopédie Informatique, 2009

3- François Sicot, Health with an open heart, 2011

4- Le petit Larousse illustré 2009,

5- Mukedi Diesta-Mputu D., - The organisation of a service

IT in a management/company system, EUE, Chisinau, Moldova, Europe 2024

- Mental Poverty, a "rampant" nuclear weapon, EUE, Chisinau, Moldova, Europe 2024

- Computer networks :

the world in our hands, EUE, Chisinau, Moldova, Europe 2024

- Some major resolutions in professional difficulties in IT management, EUE, Chisinau, Moldova, Europe 2024

Other sources

- Wikipedia
- www.universalis.fr< encyclopaedia
- Logic bomb, CommentCaMarche.net
- Lemag.ird.fr, Jean Jacques Muyembe, 29/08/24 at 15h43.
- Computer jargon
- http://www. kav.ch/avpve/wo rms/ema i l/klez.stm

TABLE OF CONTENTS

Printed by Books on Demand GmbH, Norderstedt / Germany